What DO YOU THINK?

WHAT SHOULD WE DO ABOUT HOMELESSNESS?

BY RAYMIE DAVIS

Gareth Stevens PUBLISHING

Please visit our website, www.garethstevens.com. For a free color catalog of all our high-quality books, call toll free 1-800-542-2595 or fax 1-877-542-2596.

Library of Congress Cataloging-in-Publication Data
Names: Davis, Raymie, author.
Title: What should we do about homelessness? / by Raymie Davis.
Description: New York, NY : Gareth Stevens Publishing, [2023] | Series: What do you think? | Includes index. | Audience: Grades 2-3
Identifiers: LCCN 2021044867 (print) | LCCN 2021044868 (ebook) | ISBN 9781538278833 (paperback) | ISBN 9781538278857 (library binding) | ISBN 9781538278840 (set) | ISBN 9781538278864 (ebook)
Subjects: LCSH: Homelessness–Juvenile literature. | Homeless persons–Services for–Juvenile literature. | Housing policy–Juvenile literature.
Classification: LCC HV4493 .D387 2023 (print) | LCC HV4493 (ebook) | DDC 362.5/92–dc23/eng/20211206
LC record available at https://lccn.loc.gov/2021044867
LC ebook record available at https://lccn.loc.gov/2021044868

First Edition

Portions of this work were originally authored by Emma Jones and published as *Why Are Some People Homeless?* All new material in this edition authored by Raymie Davis.

Published in 2023 by
Gareth Stevens Publishing
29 East 21st Street
New York, NY 10010

Editor: Caitie McAneney
Designer: Michael Flynn

Photo credits: Cover, p. 1 Rawpixel/Shutterstock.com; back cover and series background MYMNY/Shutterstock.com; p. 5 Followtheflow/Shutterstock.com; p. 7 M_Agency/Shutterstock.com; p. 9 Mongkolchon Akesin/Shutterstock.com; p. 10 Mega Pixel/Shutterstock.com; p. 11 Prostock-studio/Shutterstock.com; p. 13 Pressmaster/Shutterstock.com; p. 15 Monstar Studio/Shutterstock.com; p. 17 tommaso79/Shutterstock.com; pp. 18–19 SpeedKingz/Shutterstock.com; p. 21 addkm/Shutterstock.com.

Printed in the United States of America

CPSIA compliance information: Batch #CSGS23: For further information contact Gareth Stevens, New York, New York at 1-800-542-2595.

CONTENTS

WORDS IN THE GLOSSARY APPEAR IN **BOLD** TYPE THE FIRST TIME THEY ARE USED IN THE TEXT.

PEOPLE WITHOUT A HOME

Think about your home. What do you have there? Many people have food, care, and safety at home. But millions of Americans, including families and children, experience homelessness. They live in **shelters**, in cars, and sometimes on city streets because they don't have a home of their own.

People argue over the best ways to help people experiencing homelessness. First, you need to know why people don't have homes. That can help you make an informed opinion about how to help.

Think ABOUT IT!

THE U.S. DEPARTMENT OF HOUSING AND URBAN DEVELOPMENT FOUND THAT IN JANUARY 2020, MORE THAN 580,000 PEOPLE EXPERIENCED HOMELESSNESS ON JUST ONE NIGHT.

IT'S IMPORTANT TO HAVE ALL THE FACTS WHEN TRYING TO TALK ABOUT THIS TOUGH TOPIC.

BE INFORMED

Some groups believe that people are homeless because of their own poor choices. Some people see those who are homeless as **criminals**. They may think those people are always dangerous, or unsafe.

However, homeless people are still people, and all people should be treated with understanding. People who are homeless have often faced hard times in their lives that forced them into a shelter or onto the streets. Uninformed views of homelessness are harmful to people going through it. People experiencing homelessness are sometimes even **attacked**.

Think ABOUT IT!

SOME PEOPLE THINK THOSE WHO ARE HOMELESS ARE LAZY. BUT 25 PERCENT OF ADULTS IN HOMELESS FAMILIES HAVE AT LEAST ONE JOB.

PEOPLE WHO EXPERIENCE HOMELESSNESS WHILE HAVING A JOB ARE SOMETIMES CALLED THE "WORKING HOMELESS."

LIVING IN POVERTY

People living in **poverty** don't have enough money to provide for their basic needs, like housing and food. Many people living in poverty are one unlucky event away from losing their home. One of the leading causes of homelessness is not having enough income, or money coming in.

Sometimes people need the money they use to pay for their home for something unexpected. This can include medical bills or a car accident. Some people say that a higher **minimum wage** and jobless **benefits** can help.

Think ABOUT IT!

ABOUT 9.6 MILLION AMERICANS LOST THEIR JOB DURING THE COVID-19 **PANDEMIC** IN 2020.

PEOPLE LOSE THEIR INCOME WHEN THEY LOSE A JOB.

NO AFFORDABLE HOUSING

Some people can't afford a home to live in. In recent years, the cost of rent has been rising in the United States. At the same time, the number of affordable housing units has fallen. These two things can lead to homelessness when they're combined.

When people can't make payments on their home, something called foreclosure can happen. This is when a person loses the right to their home because they can't make the payments on it. People have to leave their homes. Renters can be evicted, or forced to leave their homes, if they can't make payments.

Think ABOUT IT!

IN EVERY U.S. STATE, RENTAL COSTS ARE HIGHER THAN THE INCOME MADE FROM THE HOURLY MINIMUM WAGE.

PEOPLE ARGUE THAT MORE LOW-INCOME HOUSING AND GOVERNMENT HELP WITH HOUSING COSTS CAN KEEP MORE PEOPLE IN THEIR HOMES.

DEALING WITH MENTAL ILLNESS

Some people suffer from illnesses and **disabilities** that lead to homelessness. This is especially true of mental illness.

Mental illnesses often cause people to become unable to take care of themselves and their home. They also cause people to push away those who might help keep them from becoming homeless. People who are in danger of becoming homeless often don't have access to good mental health care. Better mental health services can help people who are experiencing homelessness.

Think ABOUT IT!

*THE UNITED STATES HAS A LARGE HOMELESS **VETERAN** POPULATION. VETERANS OFTEN SUFFER MENTAL HEALTH ISSUES AFTER RETURNING FROM WAR.*

PEOPLE WITH SEVERE MENTAL ILLNESS NEED TREATMENT, SUCH AS MEDICINES AND TALKING TO A PROFESSIONAL.

HARMFUL DRUGS

Not every person who is homeless uses drugs and alcohol. Many do not. However, **substance abuse**, such as drug and alcohol abuse, is a leading cause of homelessness, especially for single adults.

Substance abuse costs money, which could be used to pay for housing. It can also cause people to lose their job and push away loved ones, which could lead to homelessness. In some cases, people begin abusing drugs and alcohol after they become homeless. It often makes their problems worse.

SUBSTANCE ABUSE AND MENTAL ILLNESS OFTEN ARE SEEN TOGETHER IN HOMELESS POPULATIONS.

RUNNING AWAY

Some people need to leave their home for their safety. They might have experienced **violence** at home. About 12 percent of the homeless population in the United States is made up of survivors of domestic violence, which is violence that happens in the home.

Women suffer from domestic violence more often than men. These women often don't have access to the money they'd need for housing. They sometimes have nowhere else to go but shelters. Many women have to bring their children with them to the shelters.

Think ABOUT IT!

MORE THAN 30 PERCENT OF WOMEN AND 25 PERCENT OF MEN HAVE EXPERIENCED DOMESTIC VIOLENCE.

PEOPLE CAN STAY IN HOMELESS SHELTERS AND WOMEN'S SHELTERS UNTIL THEY FIND HOUSING AWAY FROM THEIR ABUSER.

YOUNG PEOPLE WITHOUT HOMES

Many people imagine single adults when they think of homeless people. But children and young adults also experience homelessness. In some cases, they run away from home and have nowhere else to go. In other cases, their family kicks them out of the house.

A large number of homeless young people were part of the foster care system. They were cared for by someone other than their parent for a period of time. When they turned 18, they may have had nowhere to go.

MANY YOUNG PEOPLE DON'T WANT TO ADMIT THEY DON'T HAVE A HOME, SO THEY MAKE IT SEEM AS IF THEY'RE NOT HOMELESS.

THE BEST WAY TO HELP

There are many reasons why people experience homelessness, such as losing a job or having a mental illness. Understanding all these reasons helps people form educated points of view about homelessness and how to help those who live without a home. Many people call for better mental health services, more low-income housing, and more programs for young people without homes.

You can help the homeless in your community by **volunteering** at a shelter or giving food, clothing, and blankets.

What do you think is the best way for you to help?

BELIEFS ABOUT THE HOMELESS POPULATION

FALSE	TRUE
- ALL HOMELESS PEOPLE ARE LAZY.	- MANY PEOPLE EXPERIENCING HOMELESSNESS HAVE AT LEAST ONE JOB, SOMETIMES MORE.
- ALL HOMELESS PEOPLE ARE VIOLENT.	- PEOPLE EXPERIENCING HOMELESSNESS ARE MORE LIKELY TO BE THE VICTIM OF AN ATTACK.
- ALL HOMELESS PEOPLE LIVE OUTSIDE.	- PEOPLE EXPERIENCING HOMELESSNESS ALSO LIVE IN CARS, SHELTERS, OR OTHER TEMPORARY HOUSING.
- ALL HOMELESS PEOPLE ARE SINGLE ADULTS.	- THIRTY PERCENT OF PEOPLE WHO ARE HOMELESS ARE CHILDREN OR PART OF A FAMILY UNIT.

YOU CAN VOLUNTEER AT A SOUP KITCHEN TO GIVE FOOD TO PEOPLE WHO NEED IT.

GLOSSARY

attack: to try to harm someone or something

benefit: financial help in time of sickness, old age, or unemployment

criminal: a person who is guilty of a crime

disability: something that limits a person's ability to do certain tasks or actions necessary for daily life

minimum wage: the lowest amount of money a person can be paid per hour of work

pandemic: an outbreak of disease that occurs over a wide geographic area and affects a great proportion of the population

poverty: the state of being poor

shelter: a place that offers food and housing to those in need

substance abuse: the misuse of a drug

veteran: someone who was in the military

violence: the use of force to harm someone

volunteer: to do a job without pay

FOR MORE INFORMATION

BOOKS

Brooks, Gene. *Poverty and Our Future.* New York, NY: PowerKids Press, 2022.

Hyde, Natalie. *Housing and Homelessness.* New York, NY: Crabtree Publishing, 2022.

Roberts, Dr. Jillian. *On Our Street: Our First Talk About Poverty.* Olympia, Washington: Orca Book Publishers, 2018.

WEBSITES

Be a Volunteer
kidshealth.org/en/kids/volunteering.html#catpeople
Learn how you can volunteer in your community!

Going to a Therapist
kidshealth.org/en/kids/going-to-therapist.html#catpeople
Talking to a professional about mental health is helpful for people of all ages. Check out how therapists can help in this resource.

How Kids Can Help the Homeless
medium.com/@hccb/how-kids-can-help-homeless-8adca96a87dc
Find some ideas about how you can help the homeless, with help from your parent or guardian.

Publisher's note to educators and parents: Our editors have carefully reviewed these websites to ensure that they are suitable for students. Many websites change frequently, however, and we cannot guarantee that a site's future contents will continue to meet our high standards of quality and educational value. Be advised that students should be closely supervised whenever they access the internet.

INDEX